This Book Belongs To

....

G000123256

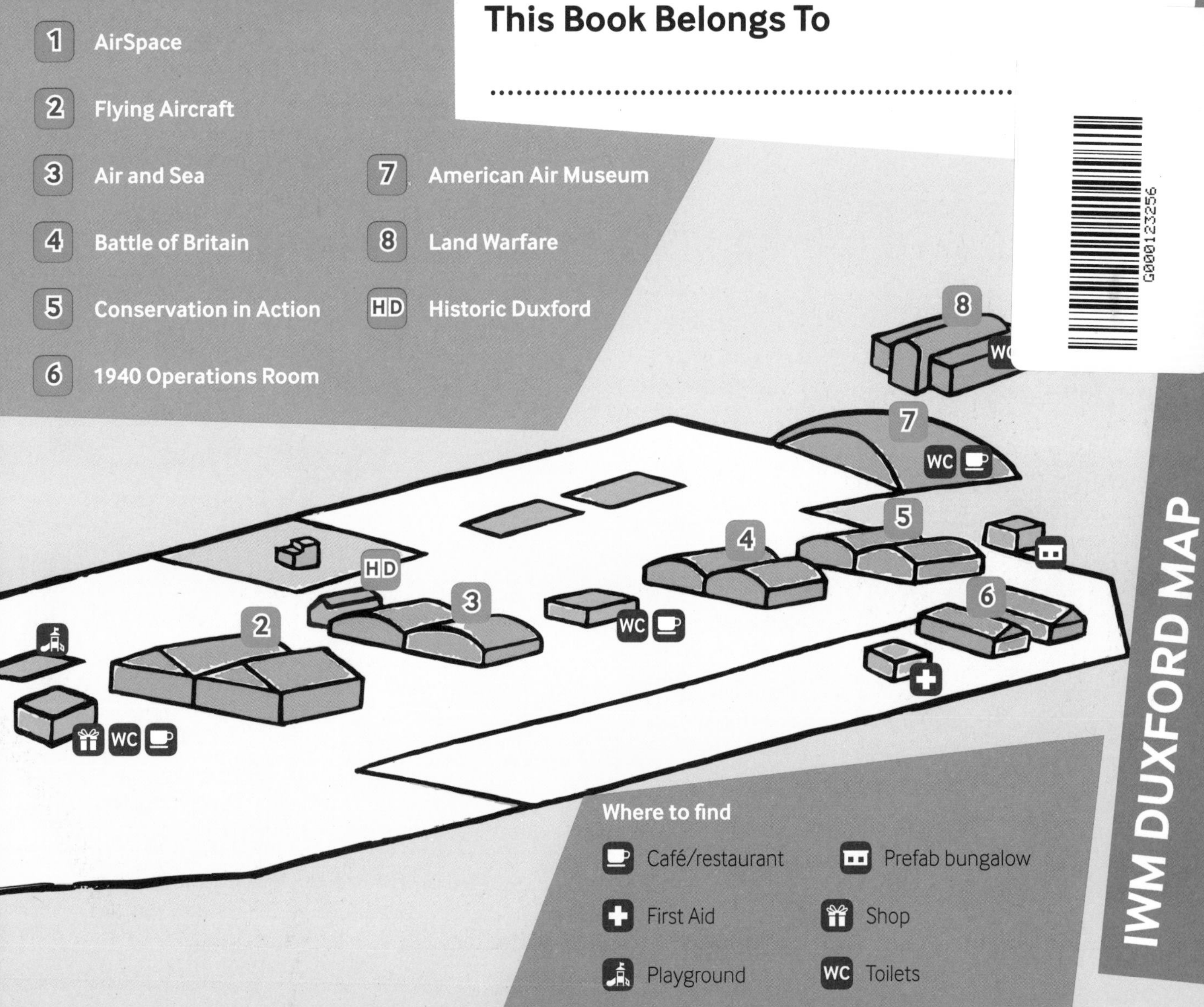

IWM DUXFORD MAP

WELCOME

Welcome to IWM Duxford! There's so much to see on this huge site, which has become many different things over the years. IWM Duxford is the first home of the Spitfire; a working airfield; a store for IWM's large objects; an air museum; a historic community all of its own; and a fantastic space to explore.

What will IWM Duxford be to you?

IWM Duxford is a big place. Don't try to see it all in one visit!

Look out for these features in your guidebook:

- The 'Find It' tag, showing you special things to look out for on your visit

- Sticker activities, using the stickers at the back of this book

- 'Start a Conversation': questions to get you talking with your family about what you've seen (there are helpful hints for grown-ups on page 30)

- 'Fun Facts' to boggle your mind and impress your friends

- 'My Duxford': stories from the people who have lived and worked here over the years

- Activities to do either during your visit, or later on at home

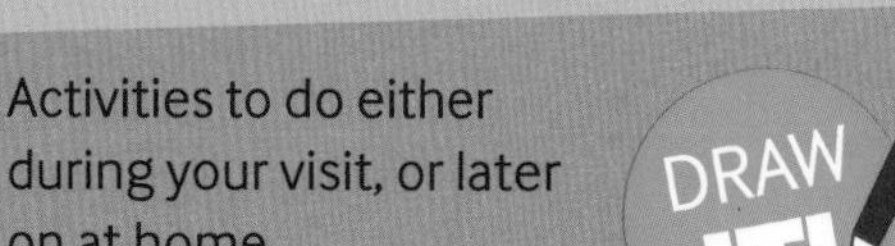

CONTENTS

AIRSPACE

Before aeroplanes were invented, the word 'plane' meant a flat surface. An 'aeroplane' was a flat wing that could lift something into the air. Later, 'aeroplane' came to mean the aircraft itself.

Early pioneers experimented with one flat surface (a monoplane), two (a biplane) or even three or four. By the First World War, biplanes were most popular – like the DH9 biplane here in AirSpace. The DH9 was one of the first kinds of aircraft to be flown from IWM Duxford.

A wing works because of the difference in air pressure between the air travelling over the top of the wing and the air that is pushed underneath. The lower pressure air passing on top of the wing surface 'sucks' the wing upwards.

DH9

FIND IT!

This tiny red aircraft is operated by radio controls. Called the Northrop SD-1, it was used to take photos of battlefields in the 1960s. With no-one inside it, people didn't have to risk their lives flying low over the enemy.

Because digital cameras hadn't been invented, the pictures had to be developed from film in a darkroom. Can you find the mobile darkroom (the ATREL A1 Processing Cabin) near the SD-1?

This small plane, hanging up high in AirSpace, is called an RE8. It was used to take pictures of the battlefield in the First World War to show the British guns where they should be firing.

It wasn't easy. Cameras were much bigger than they are today, and sitting in an RE8 was uncomfortable. There was no safety glass, so the cockpit was open. A flight in an RE8 could be cold, wet – and very windy!.

Most Second World War pilots learned to fly in a Tiger Moth biplane like this one. Yellow was thought to be the best colour for making a plane visible, so that anyone flying nearby could see it coming. But tests now show that black is the colour which stands out best against the sky in daytime.

In modern jet engines, like this Rolls-Royce Trent 800 aero-engine, blades or giant fans push air into the engine where it's heated by burning fuel. The hot air shoots out backwards, pushing the aircraft forwards with much more force than the old-style piston engine.

Concorde was a passenger jet aeroplane which could fly at twice the speed of sound. Duxford's Concorde is only open at certain times – check them at the beginning of your visit if you want to see inside!

FIND IT!

This Jeep is attached to crash pans, ready to be dropped by parachute from an aircraft. The parachute is designed to detach as soon as the Jeep hits the ground, so it won't be damaged by being dragged along. Can you spot the four parachutes?

THE LANCASTER UP CLOSE

The Lancaster was mainly used for bombing raids at night, when its dark colour helped camouflage it against the sky. But the tips of the propeller are painted bright yellow! This was to make sure that people didn't accidentally walk into the spinning blades when it was getting ready for take-off.

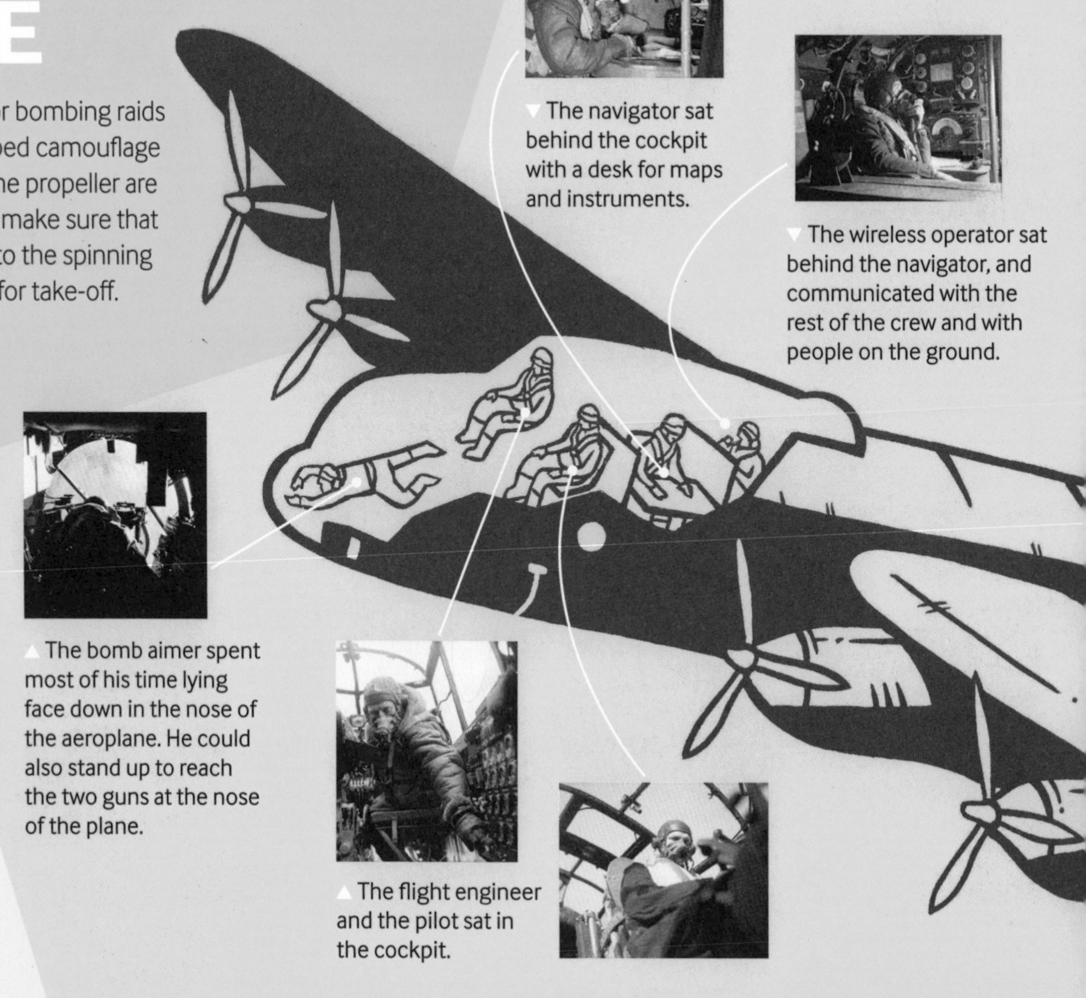

▼ The navigator sat behind the cockpit with a desk for maps and instruments.

▼ The wireless operator sat behind the navigator, and communicated with the rest of the crew and with people on the ground.

▲ The bomb aimer spent most of his time lying face down in the nose of the aeroplane. He could also stand up to reach the two guns at the nose of the plane.

▲ The flight engineer and the pilot sat in the cockpit.

'As the bomb aimer I was right up in the nose where I had absolutely no heating. What heating there was in the Lancaster was blown directly into the pilot's compartment.'

Donald Falgate, bomb aimer with 49 Squadron, RAF, in the Second World War

Which crew member would you rather be?

Start a Conversation

The Allied bombing campaign, using aircraft like the Lancaster, destroyed cities and killed hundreds of thousands of people – but it made a huge contribution to defeating Hitler. Do you think it can be worth bombing cities to win a war?

The mid-upper gunner sat in the gun turret, where he could see all around and use his two guns to aim forwards and sideways.

The rear gunner sat in a tiny turret in the plane's tail and operated four guns.

Top speed: 270 mph

Flight range: 1,160 miles (to Germany and back)

Wing span: 31m

Length: 21m

Height: 5.94m

Bomb load: 6,350kg

Costumed guide in AirSpace, standing underneath the Lancaster

THE AIRFIELD

Duxford's airfield has been the scene of take-offs, landings, accidents and drama ever since the First World War. It's still a busy working airfield today, where you can see vintage aircraft flying.

Airfields were originally just that – fields covered in grass. Aeroplanes took off in different directions depending which way the wind was blowing. In Duxford's early days, sheep were allowed to nibble the grass to keep it short! The first runway was built during the Second World War to cope with heavier planes, but we still use the word 'airfield' today.

Gloster Grebes at Duxford in 1927

FIND IT!

In summer, there are four fire trucks on duty, and in winter there are three. You'll probably spot them near the Control Tower. They need to respond quickly to an incident on the airfield.

ALAN DANIELS

Alan Daniels is IWM Duxford's Senior Airfield Fire Officer. Because it is a working airfield, IWM Duxford has its own permanent fire crew of 13 people who deal with aircraft and vehicle accidents. The crews respond to medical emergencies and look after fire safety for all of IWM's branches. Like all fire crews, IWM Duxford's fire fighters sometimes get called out to minor emergencies like saving a cat that's stuck up a tree ... or once, Alan remembers, rescuing a bird that was stuck up a tree!

FIND IT!

In the concrete at the front of Hangar 2 is a secret message. Two RAF squadrons were stationed at IWM Duxford during the Cold War – 64 and 65 Squadron. If you look very hard, you can see a scarab beetle scratched into the concrete (we've added a white outline). This was 64 Squadron's symbol.

Air shows have been staged at Duxford since the 1920s, and they are still very popular today. Thousands of visitors come to see historic planes flying, to watch display teams doing aerobatics, and to enjoy entertainment from musicians and living history groups.

Fun Fact

The rival squadrons liked to play silly tricks on each other. One morning, 64 Squadron were lining up their aeroplanes ready for the day. But every time they brought a plane up, the last one had vanished! Sneakily, 65 Squadron had been towing their planes to the other side of the airfield and hiding them.

JOHN ROMAIN

Lots of people envy John Romain. He runs the Aircraft Restoration Company (ARC), and part of his job is to fly the historic aircraft which ARC maintains at IWM Duxford. John fell in love with historic planes like Messerschmitts and Spitfires as a young boy watching the film *Battle of Britain*, which was partly filmed at IWM Duxford. Later, he trained as an engineer, volunteered at IWM Duxford, and learned to fly. John has flown more than 100 different types of vintage aircraft, and he's flown over 1000 hours just in Spitfires.

At the heart of the airfield is the Control Tower. It was built in the Second World War, to allow a view over the field and to house new radio equipment for keeping pilots in touch with ground control. Originally there was a Watch Office (now reconstructed in the Historic Duxford hut) where an officer would be stationed while flying duties were going on.

Start a Conversation

Ask the person you're with about the first time they flew in a plane. Was it fun? Were they comfortable? Were they frightened?

FLIGHT OF THE BARBER

AT DUXFORD IN THE 1950S, FIGHTER PILOT LES MILLGATE AGREED TO TAKE THE STATION BARBER UP IN A GLOSTER METEOR FOR HIS FIRST EVER FLIGHT.

LES TRIED A COUPLE OF LOOPS AND ROLLS. EACH TIME THE BARBER WANTED TO KNOW THE NAMES OF THE MANOEUVRES.

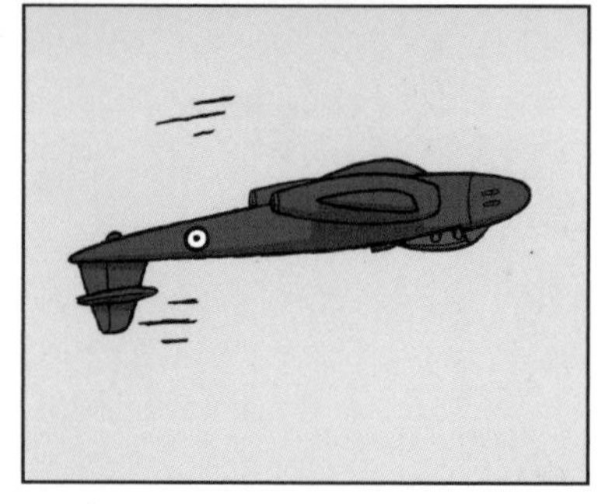

SUDDENLY, SOMETHING WENT WRONG, AND THE METEOR WAS SPINNING UPSIDE DOWN AND OUT OF CONTROL.

TERRIFIED, LES FOUGHT TO GET THE PLANE THE RIGHT WAY UP. AS HE REGAINED CONTROL, HE HEARD A VOICE...

STARRING... IWM DUXFORD

Film and TV crews regularly film at IWM Duxford, using historic aircraft and military vehicles as well as wartime locations. Films starring Duxford include *Memphis Belle* (1990), *The Monuments Men* (2014) and *Dunkirk* (2017).

Fun Fact

Three First World War aircraft hangars still exist at IWM Duxford – but one is missing.

In 1968, Duxford was used as a location for the film *The Battle of Britain*. The crew needed to film an explosion ... so they blew up a whole hangar! The film did more damage to IWM Duxford than any Second World War air raid.

The missing hangar was known as the 'theatre hangar'. It was used for fun events like dances, concerts, boxing and roller-skating. The photo shows a band of US airmen, 'The Thunderbolts', playing in the hangar in the 1940s.

THE STORY OF DUXFORD

1917–18: An airfield is built at Duxford, to train pilots from the Royal Flying Corps.

1 April 1918: The new Royal Air Force (RAF) and Women's Royal Air Force (WRAF) take over from the Royal Flying Corps. Duxford becomes an RAF station.

November 1918: The First World War ends. Flying stops at Duxford in 1919.

1920: RAF Duxford reopens for pilot training. The RAF shares Duxford's airfield with the University Air Squadron flying club, from nearby Cambridge University.

1924: Duxford becomes an RAF fighter station.

1938: The first Supermarine Spitfire is delivered to the RAF at Duxford. The Spitfire will become one of the most famous aircraft of the Second World War.

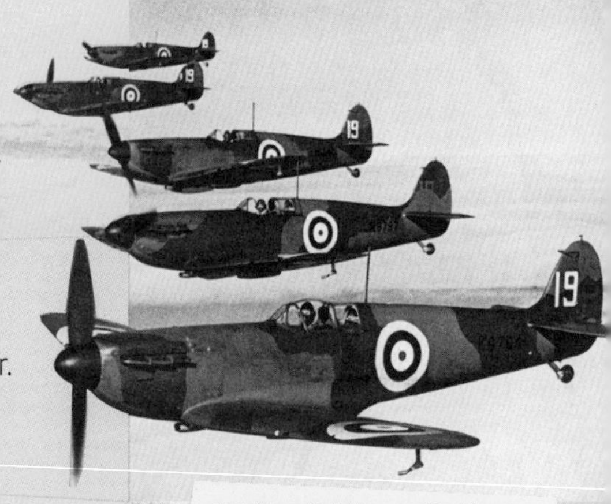

Spitfires flying over Duxford

1939: The Second World War begins. At Duxford, temporary buildings are put up in a hurry to make space for all the extra activity. Aircraft are moved to the edge of the airfield instead of in the hangars, where they would be more easily hit in an air raid.

1940: Duxford plays a key part in the Battle of Britain, when the British RAF and the German Luftwaffe fight in the skies above southern England.

April 1943: The RAF hands over Duxford to their American allies. The US Army Air Force will use the station until the end of the war.

US airmen at Duxford, drinking Coca-Cola

The Royal Flying Corps (RFC) was set up in 1912. At the start of the First World War, in 1914, it had fewer than 150 aeroplanes. By the end of the war, it had changed its name to the Royal Air Force (RAF) and had over 22,000 aircraft!

Fun Fact

1944: Duxford gets its first hard runway so that heavier aircraft can take off and land.

6 June 1944: D-Day begins the invasion of Europe to free it from Nazi occupation. Fighter planes from Duxford support the invasion force landing in Normandy.

December 1945: The Americans leave, and Duxford is returned to the RAF.

1949–1951: Duxford closes for rebuilding work to turn it into a modern fighter base, with a new concrete runway fit for aircraft fighting the Cold War.

The Cold War is the name for the time from the 1950s to the 1990s when the world's two superpowers, Russia and America, struggled for power. Both sides had nuclear weapons which could have destroyed the world if the war had turned 'hot'.

1957: The British government says it has the hydrogen bomb.

1958: CND, the Campaign for Nuclear Disarmament, is founded to protest against nuclear weapons.

1961: RAF Duxford is closed down. It was too far from the coast to intercept enemy aircraft that might come from Europe during the Cold War.

1971: The Imperial War Museum (IWM) starts to use Duxford to store large objects.

1976: IWM opens Duxford to the public as a permanent museum site.

Children at IWM Duxford's opening day, 28 June 1976

In front of the Air and Sea hangar, there is a hut called Historic Duxford. Inside, you'll find all sorts of activities to help you explore the history of IWM Duxford.

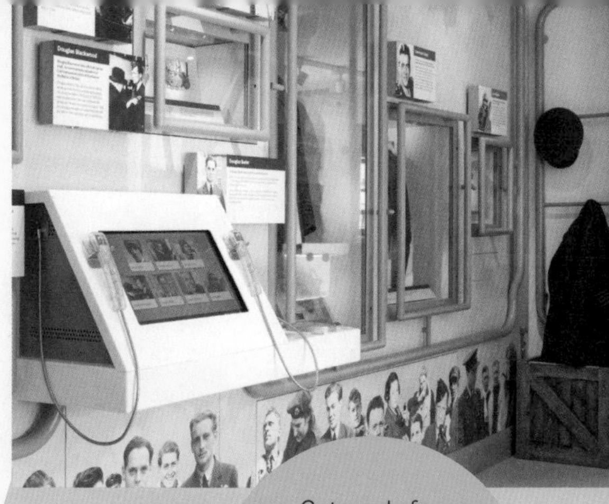

FIND IT!

Get ready for work: try on some of the uniforms from Duxford's past. Which one is your favourite?

✓

LOOK! NO HANDS!

SECOND WORLD WAR PILOT DOUGLAS BADER (RIGHT) IS FAMOUS FOR FLYING FIGHTER PLANES, DESPITE HAVING LOST BOTH HIS LEGS. JOE COX (LEFT) WAS A PILOT WITH DOUGLAS AT DUXFORD IN THE 1930s.

AFTER LOSING HIS LEGS DOUGLAS WAS BANNED FROM FLYING, BUT HIS FRIEND JOE AGREED TO TAKE HIM ON A TRAINING FLIGHT. JOE EVEN LET DOUGLAS FLY THE AEROPLANE FOR A WHILE.

JOE WAS AMAZED BY HOW WELL DOUGLAS FLEW - HE EVEN MANAGED A PERFECT LANDING. BUT NO-ONE IN THE MESS BELIEVED THAT DOUGLAS HAD FLOWN THE AEROPLANE!

SO THEY WENT UP AGAIN. DOUGLAS LANDED THE AREROPLANE, WHILE JOE KEPT HIS HANDS IN THE AIR SO EVERYONE COULD SEE IT WASN'T HIM!

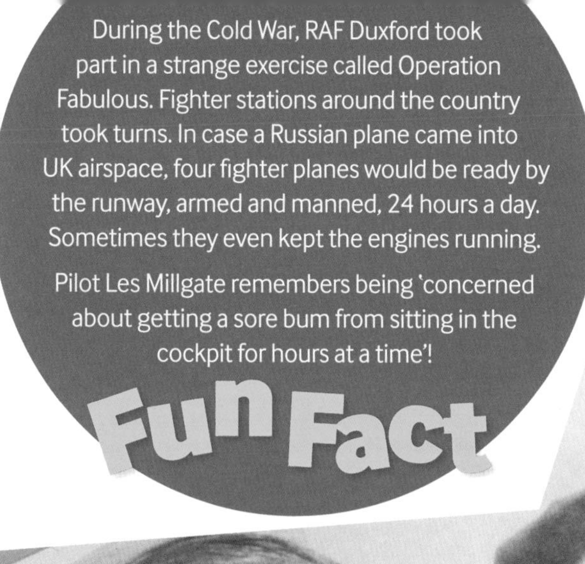

During the Cold War, RAF Duxford took part in a strange exercise called Operation Fabulous. Fighter stations around the country took turns. In case a Russian plane came into UK airspace, four fighter planes would be ready by the runway, armed and manned, 24 hours a day. Sometimes they even kept the engines running.

Pilot Les Millgate remembers being 'concerned about getting a sore bum from sitting in the cockpit for hours at a time'!

Fun Fact

MY DUXFORD: DAVID BROWN

David Brown got a taste of how many different jobs there were to do at Duxford when he did his National Service in the 1950s. He applied to be an engineer, but got a surprise when he was made a nursing assistant in the sick bay. RAF Duxford had its own ambulance, operating theatre and mortuary, and the medical staff didn't just look after pilots and ground crew: they treated everyone on site. Because one of the officers' wives was pregnant, David was even trained to deliver babies!

First World War propeller

This propeller was made as a romantic present for Muriel Vera Derby, a typist clerk who worked at Duxford in the First World War. Muriel didn't marry the man who gave this to her, but she did keep it as long as she lived. Why do you think Muriel's admirer chose a propeller to give to her?

AIR AND SEA

Like many of the aircraft in the Air and Sea hangar, this Sea Vixen fighter plane has special folding wings. This is because it was designed to go to sea on an aircraft carrier ship, where it had to fit into a small space. Aircraft carriers were widely used from the Second World War onwards.

ON TARGET

Outside the toilet block, in between Hangars 3 and 4, there are round marks on the wall. These were used in the Second World War to help members of the ground crew line up the guns on an aircraft. The guns needed to point in the right direction!

Rotor blades work just like wings. When the engine spins them round at high speed, the difference in air pressure between the top and bottom of each blade pulls the helicopter upwards. By changing the angle of the blades, the pilot can move the helicopter up, down or keep it hovering. To go forwards or backwards, the whole set of rotor blades tilts. A tail rotor stops the helicopter from spinning round, and keeps it stable.

FIND IT!

How many different animals will you find painted onto aircraft when you visit IWM Duxford?

NOSE ART

Crews painted 'nose art' like this onto their aircraft to express their team spirit and cheer themselves up.

This Sea King served with No. 814 Naval Air Squadron, who were known as 'The Flying Tigers' because of their tiger badge.

COLOUR IT!

BATTLE OF BRITAIN

The RAF's 19 Squadron was based in Hangar 4, which is now the home of the Battle of Britain exhibition. They were the first ever squadron to be issued with Spitfires, the most famous British fighter plane of the Second World War. The new aeroplanes had an astonishing top speed of 357mph! At times there are more Spitfires at Duxford than anywhere else in the world.

'The speed of the Spitfire took some getting used to. According to pilot James A Goodson of 43 Squadron, it was worth it. He said, 'It was a delight to fly ... Everybody had a love affair with the Spitfire'.

Small observer posts like this one played a vital part in the Battle of Britain. Volunteers watched for enemy and Allied aircraft, checked their height and position, and telephoned the details to the RAF. Go to the Operations Room (pages 22–23) to find out what happened to this important information.

The Germans used V1 flying bombs against Britain in revenge for the Allied bombings of Germany. V1s were fired from a steam-powered ramp, and flew to their target using internal motors, exploding when they hit the ground. The large sand-coloured object in the photo below is a dummy bomb, filled with concrete to weigh the same as a real V1. It was used to test new firing ramps.

This ambulance started out as a private car, owned by Thomas Bata who ran the Bata shoe factory in Essex. He had the car converted into an ambulance for his factory when the war began, as he expected there would be air raids.

People say 'Chocks away!' to mean 'Let's go!' But what is a chock?

It's a block of wood used to keep something steady. Wedged under an aeroplane's wheel, it works as a brake. Pilots would shout 'Chocks away!' to tell the ground crew to remove the chocks so they could take off.

Fun Fact

SPOT THE DIFFERENCE

During the Battle of Britain, the RAF used two different single-seat fighter aeroplanes. The Spitfire is the most famous, but the Hurricane was the main fighter aeroplane in the battle. When you see them flying at IWM Duxford, it is sometimes difficult to tell the difference between them. The pictures here will help you!

- The Spitfire has a long straight nose, whereas the Hurricane's nose is rounder. Can you see, in the side-on drawings, that the Hurricane's nose is rounder and shorter?
- The wings are slightly different shapes.
- The Spitfire's tail is smaller. You can see the difference more clearly when you look at the side-on drawings.

Now turn to page 21 to see the shapes of four famous Second World War aeroplanes – and when you add the stickers, you'll see them all in colour!

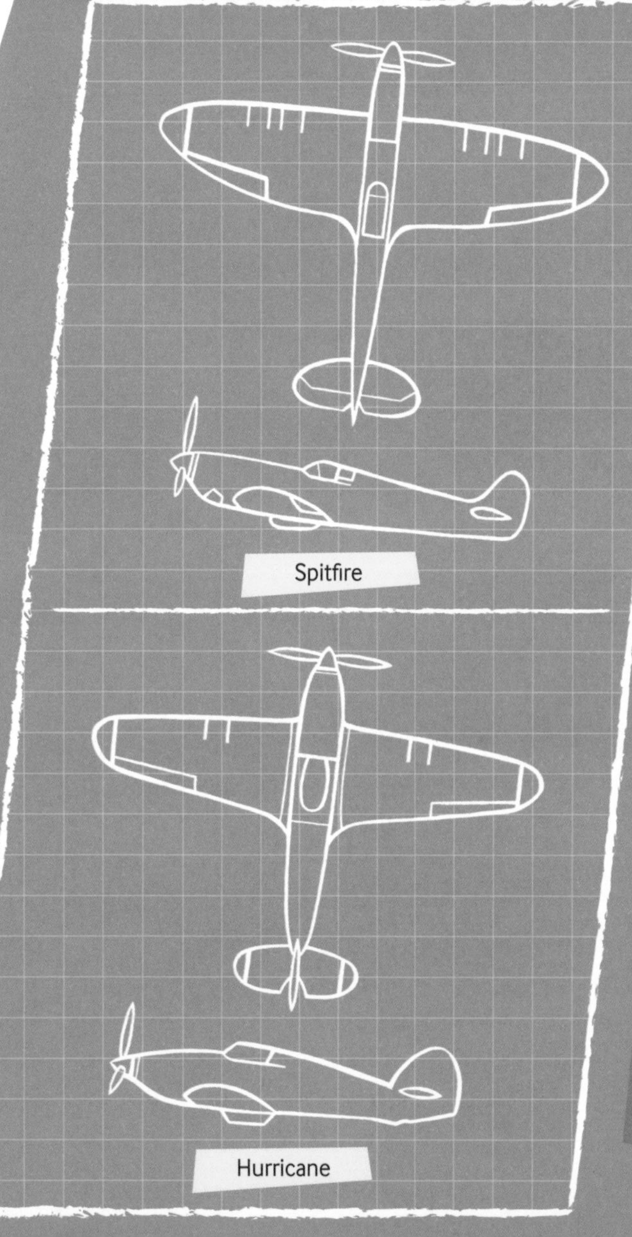

FIND IT!

In the 1930s, 19 Squadron was the first to get the new Gloster Gauntlet biplane. Gauntlets could fly for longer than the aeroplanes they replaced, but pilots sometimes forgot this. On one outing in the fog, several pilots landed early in nearby fields and walked back, thinking their aircraft could go no further. Their exasperated commander painted this huge reminder on the wall so they would have no excuse next time!

A reminder

Fun Fact

GRUMPY AND FLASH

One of Duxford's famous Battle of Britain pilots was George 'Grumpy' Unwin. Grumpy was given his nickname by Douglas Bader, after complaining about the noise Douglas made one night when he was readjusting his false legs.

Grumpy's dog Flash was a Duxford celebrity in his own right, and can be spotted in many photos from the war, including this one of Grumpy and Flash on the wing of a Spitfire.

An observer needed to be able to spot different types of aeroplanes. Practice your skills by choosing the right stickers for these silhouettes of Battle of Britain planes.

They are (1) a Messerschmitt Bf 109, (2) a Supermarine Spitfire, (3) a Heinkel He111 and (4) a Hawker Hurricane.

1940 OPERATIONS ROOM

In 1940, during the Battle of Britain, IWM Duxford's part in the battle was tracked, planned and directed from this room. Today, it's been recreated as we think it would have been in 1940.

The women in this 1940s photo of the Operations Room were called 'plotters'. They received radio reports through their headphones about Allied and enemy aircraft, and plotted the positions of the aircraft on the large map table in the centre of the room.

The clock has each 5-minute section marked in red, yellow or blue. Arrows in these colours were used on the map table to track the timing of each map position.

The Controller and his team sat on the raised platform, with the best view of the map table and all its plotted positions.

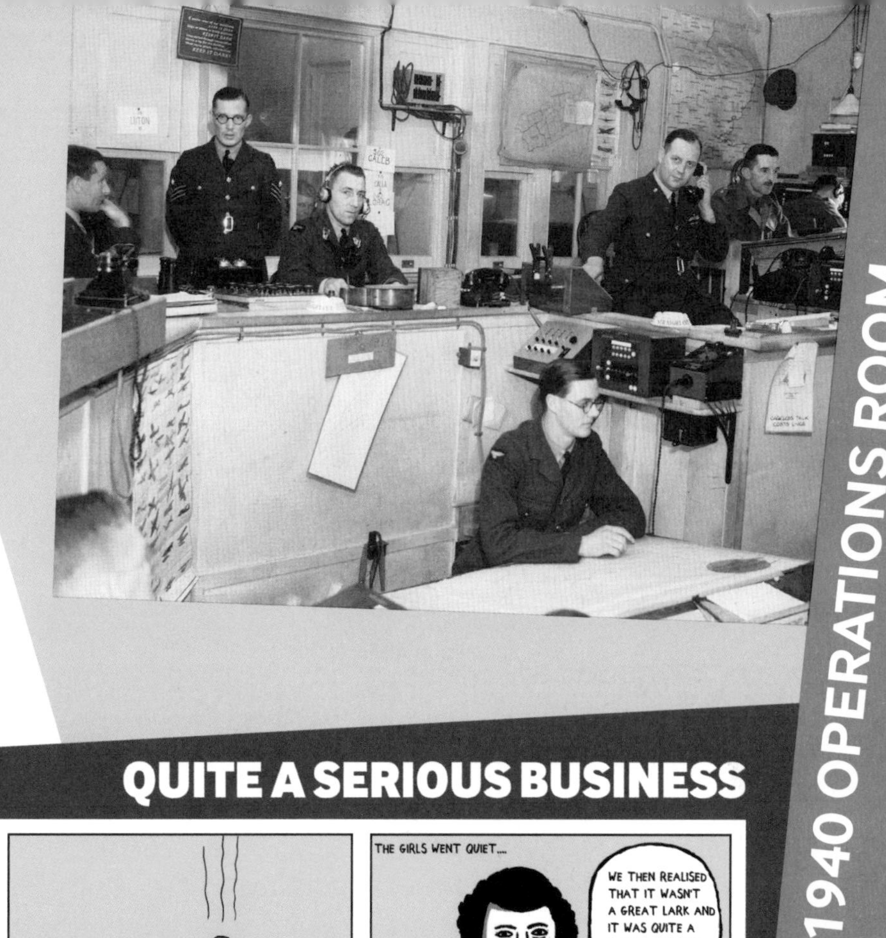

Fun Fact

Attacking German aircraft were referred to as 'bandits' by RAF pilots. When enemy aircraft were spotted by RAF fighters, the leader would shout 'Tally Ho!' (an old hunting cry) as a signal to attack.

1940 OPERATIONS ROOM

QUITE A SERIOUS BUSINESS

JEAN SWAIN WORKED AS A PLOTTER IN THE OPERATIONS ROOM. HER ARRIVAL AT DUXFORD WAS UNFORGETTABLE.

ON THE WAY, EVERYONE WAS LAUGHING AND TALKING, EXCITED ABOUT THEIR NEW ADVENTURE.

AS THEY GOT TO DUXFORD THEY SAW AEROPLANES LANDING. THEN ONE SUDDENLY STOPPED AND CRASHED TO THE GROUND.

AROUND THE SITE

Behind Hangar 4 is the old main entrance to the Duxford airfield. The big building to the left of the old entrance contained offices. The office of 'Woody' Woodhall, station commander during the Battle of Britain, was on the ground floor – where his pet dog would come and go by jumping through the window.

The old Station Headquarters

Fun Fact

WOODY'S MONOCLE

Station Commander 'Woody' Woodhall had bad eyesight, and glasses were banned for pilots flying in the RAF. But there was no rule banning monocles!

David Clark, who worked at Duxford under Woodhall, remembered that people used to find the monocle a bit unnerving: 'You always knew when he was really angry, because the monocle dropped out!'

Just past Hangar 5 are two curved huts, built in 1943 for a clever piece of technology. Inside each one was an early flight simulator called a Link trainer (named after its inventor, Edwin A Link).

In the Second World War, Link trainers were used to train pilots to fly at night. Pilots sat in the dark in the Link trainer, learning to fly using radio messages and information from a lit-up control panel. The virtual flight was plotted automatically on a map table. In the photo you can see the instructors wearing headphones, with the Link trainer in the background.

Link trainer and hut

THE HIDDEN NORTH SITE

Visitors today only see the technical and flying side of IWM Duxford. On the other side of the road, and usually closed to the public, is the rest of the site, where everyone who worked at the airfield lived. Everything they needed was there – bedrooms, mess halls for eating and socialising, a cinema, a gym, a squash court, and even a sewage works. Today, much of the North Site is used for museum storage.

Officers of the American 78th Fighter Group entertain guests in the Officers Mess at Duxford, 1940s.

FIND IT!

Opposite the old Station Headquarters is the Guard Room. Can you guess what the white hoops on the pillars were for?

In the First World War, carts that delivered goods were horse-drawn – and every RAF station needed somewhere to park the horses!

At the back of Hangar 5 is a tall tower where pilots would practise bomb aiming. The pilot sat at the top with a trigger, while on the ground below a moving table was rolled around with a map on it, made to look like the earth far below. When he sighted a target, the airman pulled the trigger.

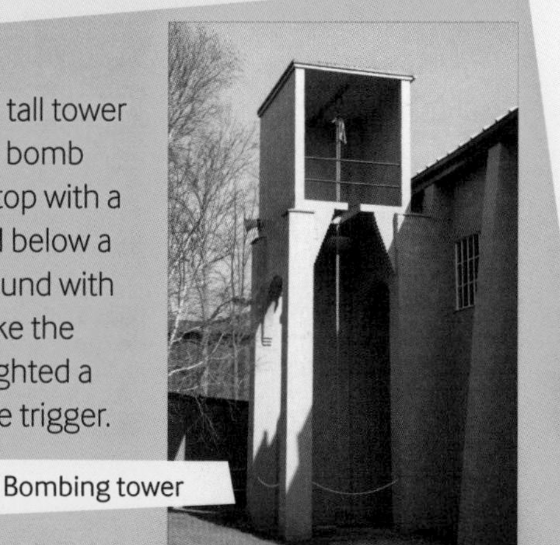

Bombing tower

THE AMERICAN AIR MUSEUM

The AAM tells the stories of men and women caught up in war, and the aircraft that served them. Three fighter squadrons of the US 8th Air Force were based at Duxford from 1943 to 1945, from where they joined American bombers in the campaign against the German air force. The P-51 Mustang and P-47 Thunderbolt became a familiar site at Duxford.

The Mustang P-51 gained huge speed and power when it was fitted with a Packard Merlin engine.

This Thunderbolt is painted with black and white stripes, just like all the aircraft used by the Allies in the Normandy invasion.

ALONE AT SEA

HUIE LAMB AND JOHN CHILDS WERE EACH FLYING MUSTANGS ON A RAID FROM DUXFORD IN 1944, WHEN SUDDENLY JOHN'S RADIO STOPPED WORKING. THEY HAD TO RELY JUST ON HUIE'S RADIO.

THEN, OVER THE SEA, HUIE'S ENGINE LOST POWER AND CAUGHT FIRE. HE MANAGED TO ESCAPE AS WATER FILLED THE COCKPIT

WITH NEITHER OF THEM HAVING RADIO CONTACT, JOHN HAD TO GO FOR HELP - LEAVING HUIE IN THE FREEZING SEA

JOHN FOUND A RESCUE PLANE IN ENGLAND AND GUIDED IT BACK TO HUIE, WHO WAS STILL HOLDING ON. HE FLEW AGAIN 10 DAYS LATER!

In the Second World War, tens of thousands of women started working in factories to build the aeroplanes needed for the war effort. Elinor Otto worked as a riveter, building aircraft in a factory in California. After the war, when the women lost their jobs, Elinor tried other work, but she soon went back to building planes. In fact, she liked it so much that she only retired in 2014 – by which time she was 95 years old!

Woman riveter in the Second World War

FASTEST!

The fastest aircraft at Duxford is also the fastest manned jet plane in the world – and it can also fly higher than any other. The Blackbird is a US spy plane with an astonishing top speed of Mach 3.31. That's more than three times the speed of sound!

Hanging up high in the AAM is the Douglas C-47 Skytrain. It has lots of rivets, as you can see in the photo. Every single one was put in by a skilled worker like Elinor.

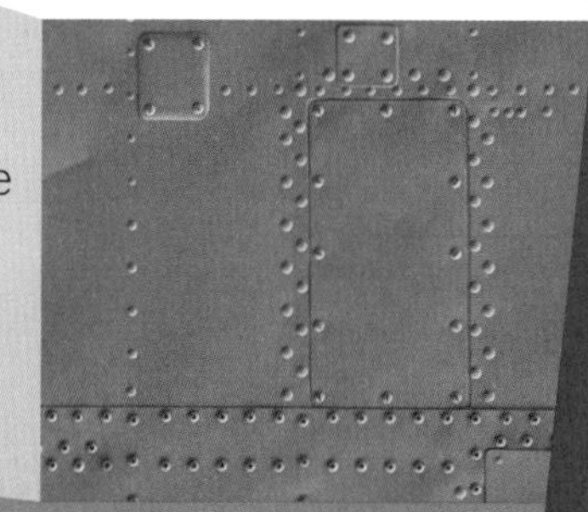

WARNING

There are lots of personal stories in the AAM. Because they relate to war, many of them are upsetting. It's always OK to choose not to read them if you don't want to.

BIGGEST!

The biggest aeroplane at Duxford is so big, you might not even see it at first. The B-52 Stratofortress bomber is in the middle of the AAM, surrounded by lots of smaller aircraft. It's 47.7m long, with a wing span of 56.4m, and it weighs 80 tonnes. That's about three times the weight of a full bin lorry!

LAND WARFARE

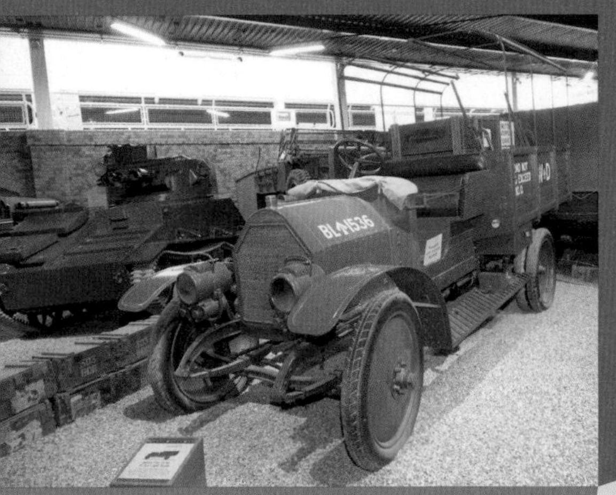

Here you can see a huge collection of tanks, trucks and artillery, and explore the Normandy Experience. Light levels are kept low to preserve the exhibits.

DUKWs are amphibious vehicles, meaning they can travel on both land and water. The Allies used DUKWs in the Second World War invasions of Sicily and Normandy. This picture, by War Artist Stephen Bone, shows DUKWs coming ashore in Normandy.

DUKWs

This is the T-34 tank, which helped Russia to defeat Germany on the Eastern Front during the Second World War. German General von Rundstedt called it the best tank in the world. It was fast, strong, and reliable in all sorts of inhospitable places.

Soviet T-34/85 Medium Tank

Fun Fact

There's another T-34 at Duxford, displayed as if it's breaking through a wall – but this one has been turned into a replica of a German Tiger tank for the film *Saving Private Ryan*.

FIND IT!

In the Normandy Experience, get your hands on some of the kit which soldiers took into battle on D-Day, including steel helmets, guns and a hand grenade.

STICKER IT!

Map Caravan

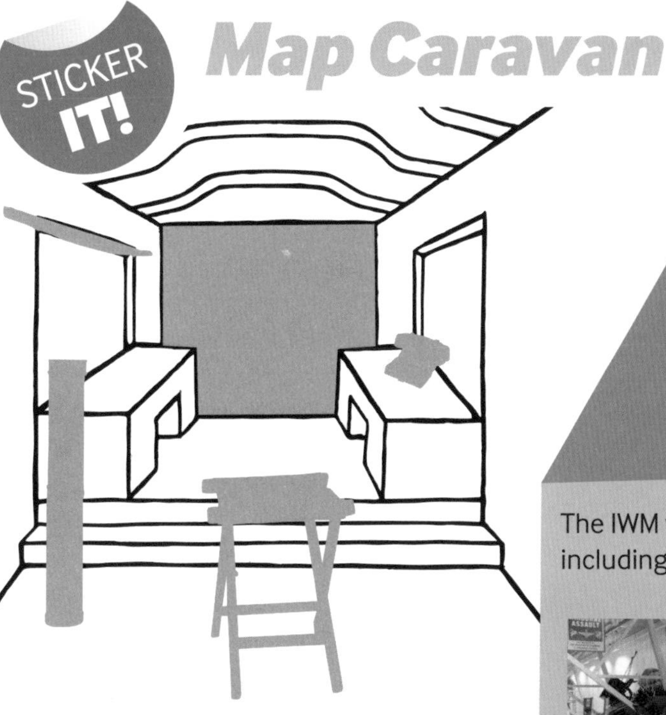

This photograph was taken in October 1944, inside the map caravan. Monty was always easy to spot, in his black beret with army badges on it. Sitting on the stool is King George VI . They are looking at a map as they discuss future battle plans.

During the Second World War, British general Bernard Montgomery, known as 'Monty', used the three caravan lorries on display in Land Warfare as his mobile base.

This drawing shows his map caravan, where he planned his campaigns. Stick in his essential kit:

- A telephone, to keep in touch
- Blackout curtains, for working at night
- A map of the battlefield
- A map case, for transporting maps
- A folding stool

The IWM works with several partner museums on site at Duxford, including these:

◀ In the AirSpace hangar, Airborne Assault has exhibits from the history of airborne forces and the Parachute Regiment, including weapons from around the world and paratroopers' kit as it changed through time.

▶ The Royal Anglian Regiment have a gallery in the Land Warfare hangar, and also a regimental memorial outside which honours members of the regiment who have been killed in service.

◀ The Duxford Aviation Society owns and maintains many non-military aircraft around the site, including famous planes like Concorde.

FOR GROWN-UPS

- IWM Duxford's size makes it a great place for children to run around and explore. It also means it can take about half an hour to walk the site from end to end, so you may want to plan your visit with this in mind.

- There are two cafés on site, near the visitor entrance and in the American Air Museum, as well as snack vans in the summer.

- Younger children can have fun climbing and flying their own planes at the playground near the Armoury café.

- Because IWM Duxford deals with stories of war, some exhibits are not suitable for young or more sensitive children, especially some of the personal stories in the American Air Museum. If your child is affected, try to find a quiet, safe space to talk about the issues later on. Ask open questions to find out what your child thinks and if they have any concerns.

- Some children find mannequins disturbing. Please note that there are mannequins in the displays in Land Warfare, Battle of Britain and Airborne Assault in particular.

OTHER IWM BRANCHES

We hope you enjoyed your visit to Duxford. For more days out exploring IWM's collections, head to our other museums.

IWM LONDON

IWM London tells the story of people's experiences of war, from the First World War to today. The museum re-opened in 2014 with a redesigned atrium and new First World War galleries.

HMS BELFAST

IWM owns a Second World War warship on the Thames in London which you can visit. Explore the nine decks to find out about life at sea and at war.

IWM NORTH

IWM's home in Manchester is housed in a dramatic building which represents how war disrupts the world. Its exhibitions tell stories from conflicts since the First World War. Climb the AirShard tower for stunning views over the city – if you dare!

CHURCHILL WAR ROOMS

This is the underground bunker in central London where Churchill's government worked during the Blitz. Find out how the Cabinet operated here in secret from 1940 to 1945, and visit the museum dedicated to Prime Minister Winston Churchill.

Published by IWM, Lambeth Road, London SE1 6HZ
1st edition, 2017

ISBN: 978-1-904897-30-9
Printed by Belmont Press, UK

The publishers will be glad to make good in future editions any error or omissions brought to their attention.

Our thanks to Jo Foster (author), Global Blended Learning (design), Frances Castle (comic strip illustrations), Darren Baxter (front cover, and drawings on pp 1, 6-7, 17, 19, 29) and all IWM Duxford staff involved in this book.

Inside front cover: IWM_2016_067_110, IWM_SITE_DUX_002472, IWM_SITE_DUX_002761, IWM_SITE_DUX_002777, IWM_SITE_DUX_002784, IWM_SITE_DUX_002719; pp 2-3: IWM_SITE_DUX_001915, IWM_SITE_DUX_000170, IWM_SITE_DUX_001656; pp 4-5: IWM_SITE_DUX_002721, IWM_SITE_DUX_001576, IWM_SITE_DUX_002716, 2010_075_8, IWM_SITE_DUX_000575, IWM_SITE_DUX_002712, IWM_SITE_DUX_002713; pp 6-7: CH_008789, CH_008971, CH_012289, CH_012288, CH_008790, CH_008795, CH_012776, IWM_SITE_DUX_001496; pp 8-9: Q_102727, photo of Alan Daniels © Alan Daniels, IWM_SITE_DUX_002737, IWM_SITE_DUX_002723, photo of John Romain © George Romain, IWM_SITE_DUX_002267; pp 10-11: photo of Les Millgate © Les Millgate, HU_041611, RTR_000028_3_A, HU_057994; pp 12-13: HU_041570 (background), CH_000019, FRE_000293, MH_021255; pp 14-15: photo of Cox and Barder © Patricia Banks, IWM_SITE_DUX_000980, IWM_SITE_DUX_000993, IWM_SITE_DUX_000969, IWM_SITE_DUX_002747, IWM_SITE_DUX_00274, photo of David Brown © David Brown; pp 16-17: IWM_SITE_DUX_002726, IWM_SITE_DUX_002732, IWM_SITE_DUX_002729, IWM_2016_008_001, IWM_SITE_DUX_002748, IWM_SITE_DUX_002872; p. 18: IWM_SITE_DUX_001571, IWM_SITE_DUX_002740, IWM_SITE_DUX_002741, 4108_170_1; p. 20: IWM_SITE_DUX_002744, CH_001343; pp 22-23: CH_001404, IWM_SITE_DUX_002774, IWM_SITE_DUX_000331, photo of Jean Swain © Diana Prades, CH_001401; pp 24-25: IWM_SITE_DUX_002751, CH_007462, CH_001386, IWM_SITE_DUX_002753, FRE 3051, IWM_SITE_DUX_002787, IWM_SITE_DUX_002752; pp 26-27: IWM_SITE_DUX_001577 (background), UPL_6609, IWM_SITE_DUX_002772, IWM_SITE_DUX_002773, H_014259, IMG_20150213_0012, IWM_SITE_DUX_002433, IWM_SITE_DUX_002771, IWM_SITE_DUX_002010; pp 28-29: DUX_2007_056_020, DUX_2007_056_005, IWM_SITE_DUX_000407, IWM_ART_LD_004370, IWM_SITE_DUX_002759, TR_002393, IWM_SITE_DUX_002715, IWM_SITE_DUX_002867, photo of Concorde © DAS; pp 30-31: IWM_SITE_DUX_002014, IWM_SITE_LAM_000498, IWM0060, IWM_SITE_BELF_000598, IWM_SITE_CWR_000207.

Answer this quiz to see how much you've found out from your visit to Duxford. Can you remember any of the answers without looking them up?

1 What do you call a plane with two sets of wings? (answer on p. 4)

....

2 Who kept IWM Duxford's grass neat in its early years? (answer on p. 8)

....

3 Why was the theatre hangar blown up in 1968? (answer on p. 11)

....

4 Which country's air force used IWM Duxford between 1943 and 1945? (answer on p. 12)

....

5 Who lost his legs but still became a famous Second World War pilot? (answer on p. 14)

....

6 Why would an aeroplane need folding wings? (answer on p. 16)

....

7 What kind of animal was Flash? (answer on p. 20)

....

8 What job did Jean Swain do in the Operations Room in 1940? (answer on p. 23)

....

9 What did 'Woody' Woodhall wear instead of glasses? (answer on p. 24)

....

10 What did Edwin A Link invent? (answer on p. 24)

....

11 What is the biggest aeroplane at IWM Duxford? (answer on p. 27)

....

12 What sort of hat was Monty famous for wearing? (answer on p. 29)

....